Whistle blower – Ken Dodd joins up with the legendary Tiller Girls for a charity soccer match at Liverpool FC's Melwood Training Ground, during the days of the great Bill Shankly

Oil drums and old tyres make a playground paradise for children in the middle of blocks of city flats, next to the Bronte Community Centre, Copperas Hill, in 1969

This Road Safety Officer was the wheel deal at West Derby Technical School, in 1961

A CELEBRATION OF PAST TIMES

WELCOME aboard the Trinity Mirror time Machine.

Liverpool Then: Volume 2 is the much-awaited sequel to our bestselling first volume. It is a trip down Merseyside's memory lane – Liverpool's long and winding roads and a visit to all our past times.

In this 84-page glossy souvenir you will see a city for all seasons and look back on the happiest days of our lives – childhood and school days.

There are flights of fancy in a sentimental section on transport in Trains, Boats and Planes – featuring Merseysiders of all ages escaping for a while but always heading home where the heart was and is.

There are photographic records illustrating a third of our lives – that time spent in work.

Sport, entertainment and some golden Mersey Memories all recapture periods in black and white, while in our minds they are in colour.

The award-winning team of photographers from the Daily Post and Echo were making history as they went about their jobs.

Brian Johnston, chief archivist on our newspapers, knows Merseyside inside and out. He has catalogued, labelled and filed images for posterity.

"It was a labour of love, "says Brian.

"It was a happy dilemma – a case of what to leave in and what to leave out."

Every picture tells a story and every caption will take you back to a place and a time.

There will be more Liverpool Then nostalgia collections in the future which will continue to speak volumes to all generations.

So sit down, relax for a while. Switch off the telly, disconnect the iPod and mobile phone.

Ignore Facebook and Twitter, for now, and just travel back to a time when a camera was all you needed to connect and feel alive.

Happy reading . . . fond remembering . . . the way we were.

Peter Grant

Read all about it . . . are the buses on strike? Commuters in 1954 are looking at photos in the broadsheet Daily Post wondering if one day they will end up in a Trinity Mirror Nostalgia special called Liverpool Then Volume 2. The young girl at the back is asking the question: "Ma, weren't there any Echos left?"

CONTENTS

Trinity Mirror Media

Editor: Peter Grant
Design & Production: Vicky Andrews
Cover Design: Zoe Bevan
Liverpool Daily Post & Echo Image Archive:
Brian Johnston

Business Development Director: Mark Dickinson
Executive Editor: Ken Rogers
Senior Editor: Steve Hanrahan
Editor: Paul Dove
Senior Art Editor: Rick Cooke
Trinity Mirror Media Marketing Executive: Claire Brown
Sales and Marketing Manager: Elizabeth Morgan
Sales and Marketing Assistant: Karen Cadman

Printed by PCP

ISBN 978-1-906802-91-2

Cover image: The long hot summer – splashing about at the Steble Fountain, William Brown Street, in 1954

It's an August morning in 1962 and the scene for a family outing to the Pier Head to feed some Liver Birds with a difference – pigeons. This pram, by the way, was the first four-wheel drive in the city

"A picnic – well, it was just sarnies and lemonade, But memories like that never fade. The brass band played songs I'd never heard, Yet mum and dad knew every melody and every single word"

All the thrills of November 5 are mirrored in the face of four-year-old Kim Wilson, 1984

Hundreds enjoy the music of the Band of the 5th Battalion, the King's Regiment, in Sefton Park in August 1955

Pooling resources – children decide to turn the model boating lake at North Park, Bootle, into an unofficial Liverpool Lido during August 1947

"Blooming lovely you are, girls," says the Scouse Eliza Doolittle flower-seller. "Yer not bad yerself, petal," says one of the fab four femme fatale shoppers in spring, 1960.

Owen Owen in Clayton Square (a store so good they named it twice) enjoys a shopping frenzy in one of their popular summertime bargain extravaganzas in 1964

Should have spent my savings and got a taxi, think these commuters waiting for a bus in Elliott Street. Three came along right after this picture was taken, in the cold January of 1961

Her conditioning – a spring day in April 1961 and an ideal chance for these office ladies to take a midday break in serene Coronation Gardens

Trees company, but where are they? School's out in Clough Lane, Speke, in August 1958 where children look as though they are guest stars in a surreal painting

A family from Bowring Park set out with skate expectations looking for the icing on a lake, on a frosty morning in 1922

"Go...
Be free as
birds.
Fly away, our
feathered
friends.
But make sure
you're
back home
for tea,
Before the
day ends"

August 1967 and three schoolboys who get their thrills from racing pigeons, George Williams, Tommy Craven and Paul Winkle. During the school holidays they collected 15 racing pigeons from their Princes Park owners and released the birds at Brunswick Dock - five minutes flying time from the loft. As usual, the birds were waiting when the boys returned

VICARS + HEATH. PRINCES PARK. H.S.

You've been framed – Kirkby kids climbing new heights with a fun new installation, a welcome playground attraction at Mill Farm estate in 1973

Top, a new playground in Whitley Gardens, Shaw Street, sees a green part of the city come alive with the sound of laughter, screams of joy and some muddy clothes in May, 1960. Bottom, Captain Kid and his crew: "I can see our house from here." Young Liverpool landlubbers become Mersey explorers for the day in 1964

"Don't want any dinner, I'll have a jam butty. I just want to meet my mates, And have a game of footy"

Premiership players form their own street-wise club in 1965, 'The Childwall Valley Estate Team'

"Three lions, Roaring to go..."

These two brave Liverpool lion-tamers climb aboard one of the historic stone figures outside St George's Hall in 1951

It was pay day for children back in 1958 and one city centre shop had a sugar rush on its new range of confectionary – lucky bags, toffees and gobstoppers

On a dummy run – Kenneth Purslow from Salisbury County Primary School with his puppet 'The Abbot', 1951

A couple take their youngster on a feeding mission at the Pier Head. Well, it was a lot cheaper than going to Trafalgar Square for the day in the 1960s

"Ere, la, are you sure you want to be a mechanic when you leave school?" Two young businessmen have a scrap...over what will fetch a few bob in 1958

Mersey Travel commuter trials in May 1946, as the South Liverpool line is checked out. Oh dib, dib, dib - it's a fun fib, it's actually an incredible Bosun's chair demonstration by the Sea Scouts of the 17th Bootle Troop at the Sefton Park Jamborette

Toddlers of Grenville Street, off Duke Street, play for a ticket to slide with visiting dignitaries, in 1968

"Dragon, fly away,
From Liverpool
to Glasgow.
Och...go
Dragon fly
There and back
In a day"

Passengers about to board a Heron aircraft at Speke in June 1955 for the inaugural flight of Dragon Airways' new Liverpool-Glasgow air service

G-A
HUNTING · CLAN

Jam-packed: Stephen Shakeshaft's portrait of Duke Street, part of a changing city centre in March 1965

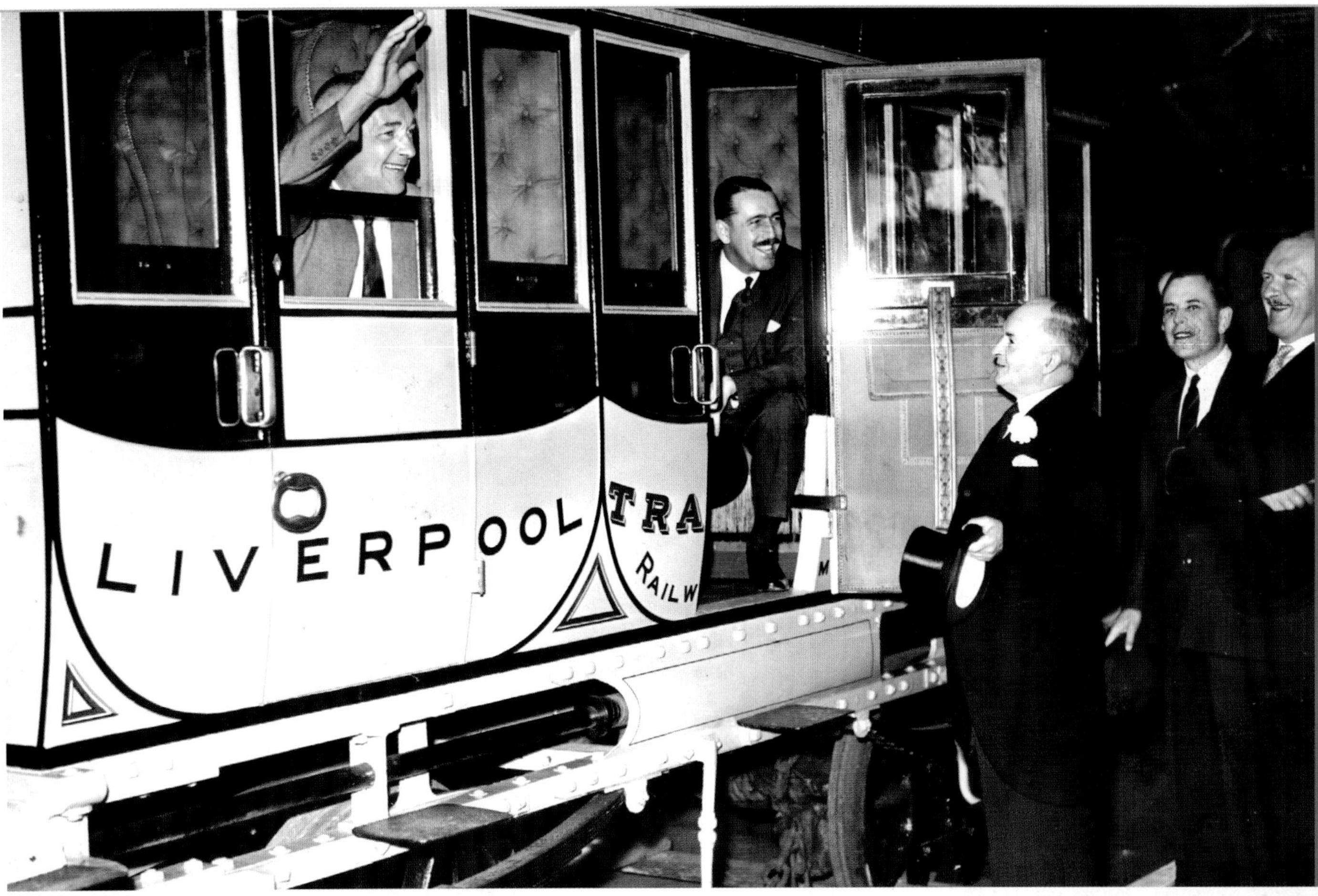

Top, one of the exhibits in the British Railways exhibition at Exchange Station in 1957, the first class carriage of the type used when the Liverpool-Manchester Railway was opened. Bottom, a day in the life of Lime Street Station captured by Stephen Shakeshaft in the 1970s

Fares please! "I took this job because I thought the change would do me good," says conductoress Ellen Tobin of Liverpool 11 – 1956

The Liverpool 'clippies' of 1956 – Audrey Cooper, Vera Hennigan, Lily Molyneux, Ellen Tobin, Doris Romano, Margaret Foster, Helene Larsen, Edna Smirk

Horse power – it is March 1943, but late enough in the century for passers-by in Church Street to stare at this carriage and pair competing with a tramcar

10B or not 10B – the transport paparazzi welcome a Green Goddess tram back to Liverpool in September 1967

"Shake, rattle and roll
through the city streets,
Steel on steel,
Where the
Mersey Sound beats"

Full steam ahead – The Isle of Man steamer Ben my Chree leaves Liverpool Landing Stage in August 1931, loaded with holiday-makers, for the last Bank Holiday of the season

All our bags are packed and ready to go – the waiting room at Princes Stage at 7am, packed full of holidaymakers waiting for the Isle of Man boat, August 1959

An Echo photographer is ambushed by fun-hungry schoolchildren on a footbridge over Northway Maghull, June 1967

"Roll on 4 o'clock,
I want to hear
the bell.
I like my teachers
and love my school.
Don't want to end up
a classroom fool.
'Cos I've got my
own stories to write
and tales to tell.
That's why I want
to hear the bell."

Okay, who's got the key? Miss D. Halliday assembles children outside Kirkby School

Portrait of artists as young men – the art room at Merchant Taylor's School, 1951

Eurovision – on a high note, the 46-strong choir of Wirral County Grammar for Girls, during rehearsals for the Montreux Choral Festival, 1969

Brought to arms – QMS Kennerley has an attentive audience of boys from Longview Secondary School as he explains how the S.L. rifle functions, 1960

Children of St Vincent's R.C. School line up in the vicinity of Park Lane, with evacuation kit, during a rehearsal in 1939

A school cruise picture to awaken happy memories – 1969 and boys and girls from Deyes Lane Secondary School, Maghull, and Maghull Grammar School, set off aboard the cruise liner Nevasa for Vigo, Tangier and Gibraltar

Playtime for these youngsters from Upton playgroup at the Victory Hall, 1967

Lip service – young pipers from Liverpool Boys' Brigade get in some practice on their chanters in 1966

In with a splash at the deep end, these youngsters from Wavertree mastered the art of swimming with the help of the Learn to Swim campaign, at Picton Road Baths. August 1974

Happy youngsters queue for the slide at Llanrwst Street playground, May 1955

"Can I have
my childhood
back?
Everything then
was in colour,
Never grey
or black.
No thoughts of
a career or a
business plan,
Just waiting in
line, at the
ice cream van"

A tasty twist on road safety in 1967

The last dinners are served at the Boys' Dinner Hour Club, Williamson Square, in 1952

"We loved clocking on, But we loved clocking off. It's all now a happy memory of the warehouse, office, canteen and factory"

Making ends meat at the Stanley Abbatoir in January 1958

Eat your heart out Willy Wonka. A veritable fruit drops feast – just one of the delicious treats served up by Taveners of Wavertree in 1969

A lunch hour scene in the spacious canteen of Evans Medical, where most of the 900 workers ate, November 1946

"These will go down a bomb", say patriotic staff at a munitions factory in 1941

Leaked to the press – workmen repair a broken water main near the junction of St Oswald Street, Prescot Road, in 1948

Workmen drinking the traditional glass of beer after the Entwistle Heights topping-out ceremony, April 1964

"On top of the world,
We'll drink to that!"

That's the drill – workers at the Littlewoods Bootle factory riveting channel track mats, used for prefabricated airstrips, in 1945

'WAIT!' warns this traffic policeman on duty at Ranelagh Street in 1967

Right: you might be excused for thinking that Bill Jones was saving for a rainy day in 1981. In the lost property office of Merseyside Passenger Transport Executive, he had more than 75 brollies in his collection, as well as shopping trollies, bags and baskets, not to mention the never-ending stream of gloves

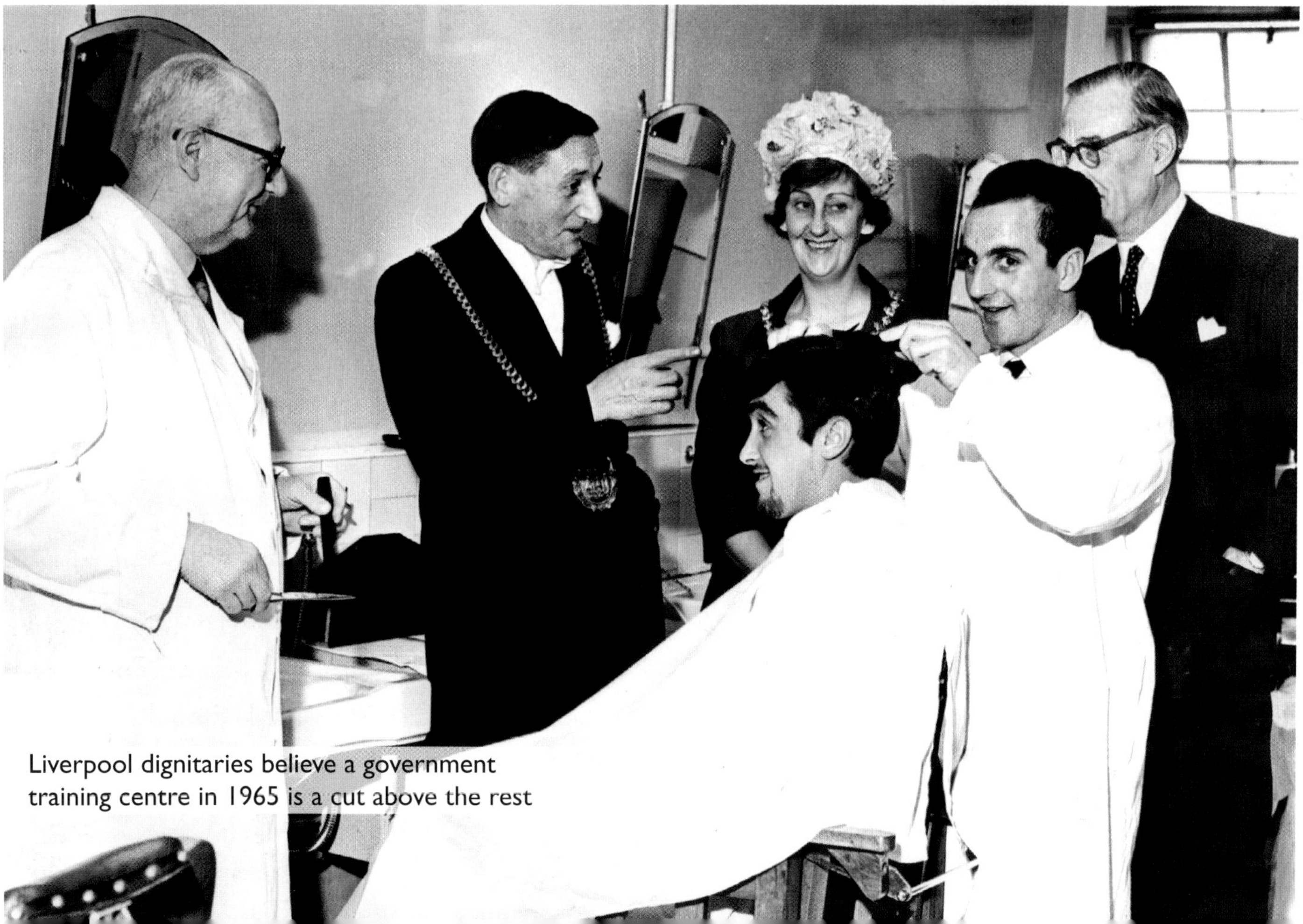

Liverpool dignitaries believe a government training centre in 1965 is a cut above the rest

De-mob happy: Liverpool soldiers, men of the First Battalion The King's Regiment, leave Freshfield for Bury St Edmunds in 1955, having served for three years in the Far East

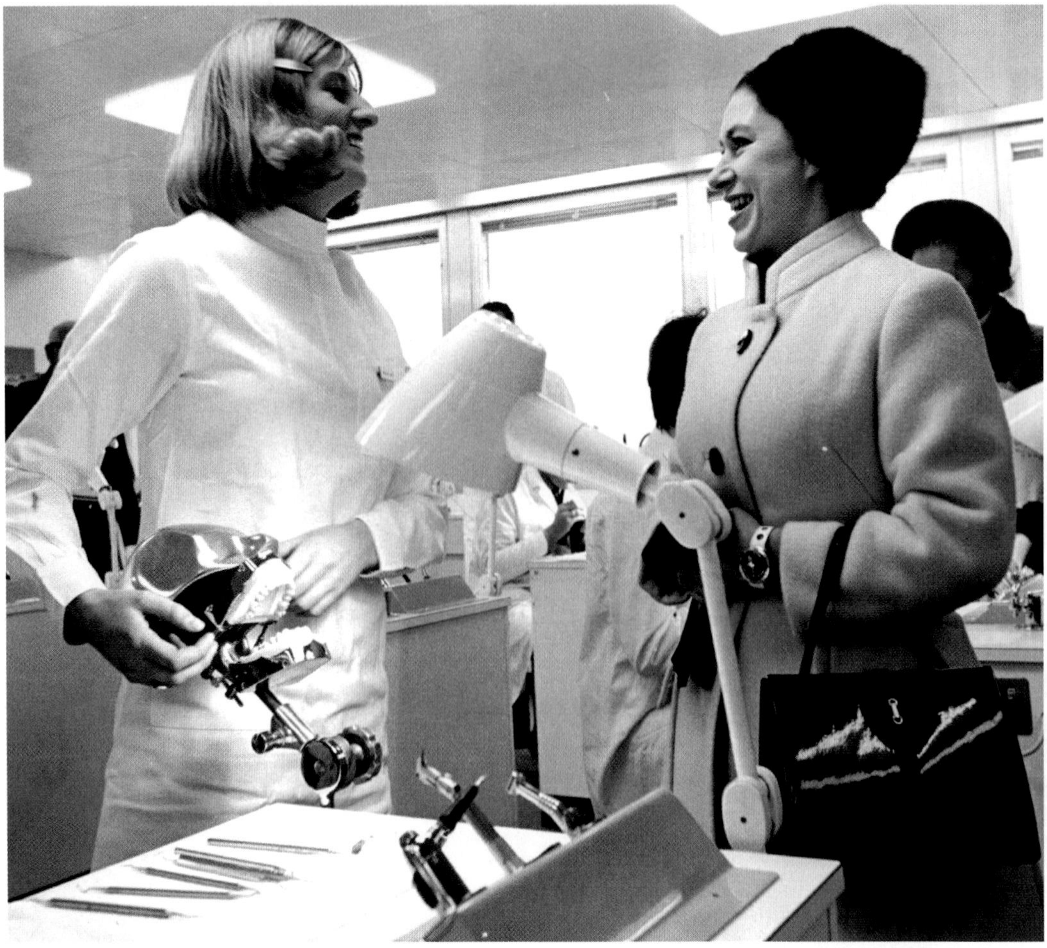

By gum . . . Wendy Conn tells the whole tooth about her dentist's degree in 1970. Princess Margaret jokes with her about the phantom 'head' on which she learns to pull and fix teeth

Stop press! Someone's stolen all the typewriters. But the show must go on as the Daily Post and Echo journalists work on scoops in Victoria Street during the 1950s

Adventurers from Huyton clubbed their short change together to go on a summer holiday. After a boozy night in a pub they came up with a perfect break: "Let's buy this taxi at the going rate, £15." They christened it Jenny and decided on a two-week tour of the South of England. The Mersey motley crew from Stockbridge Lane included: Don Marsh, Frank and Robin Foster, Ronald Arden and Bob Smith. The intrepid travellers set out on their summer holiday back in July, 1954. And they did make it back and gave themselves a tip – never again...

"Pack up our troubles,
and let's drive away.
Please God, send us
safely on our way,
We are taking a break
to Land's End
Every one of us
will end up a
life-long friend"

A great escape on the horizon, at West Kirby Boating Lake in the summer of 1955

New Brighton sands and a giggle on the donkey rides in 1945

San Tropez, the Riviera or Cannes? No, it was just a car, bus or train ride away to Southport in July 1968 – another affordable 'get-away-from-it-all' destination for many Liverpudlians

Right, said Ted: "I'm having a kip," or should that be a kipper, at Calderstones Park in July 1973

Streets ahead: Jillian Holme receives the Miss New Brighton 1971 trophy from Violet Carson – Ena Sharples from Coronation Street – with some of the other judges at the contest, including Tommy Smith, captain of Liverpool FC

Lake it easy – past times with memories of carefree days at Greenbank Park in March, 1948

The streets of the city behind them, members of Earle Road Presbyterian Youth Club enter Central Station for a ramble in Wirral – 1959

Many will recall this image of old, featuring the miniature railway at Lakeside Station, near Peter Pan's pool, in Southport

"Dreams on all these
hopeful faces,
They're off to
the National for the
world famous races..."

Under starter's orders – crowds get set for the Aintree Grand National in 1946

"War was looming but it was an odds-on certainty that the spirit of Liverpool would always be a winning trait of this great city"

'Jump Sunday' at Aintree Grand National in 1938 as famous tipster Prince Monolulu entertains the crowd

Full House!
The Royal Court Theatre received great reviews from every bingo winner in April, 1969. The star Bingo and Social Club ticked all the boxes with stunning cash prizes

Pantomime stars at a charity bowling competition in 1965 – Joe Henderson, Frankie Vaughan, Ken Dodd, Jimmy Tarbuck, Gerry Marsden

Stage fright – you can lead a donkey to the stage door but you cannot make him go through it! Lucky the donkey, from Moreton, was saved from the abattoir but made asses of her new owners after a first refusal at the Liverpool Empire in 1990. Lucky made it through to the big time to appear in Joseph and His Amazing Technicolour Dreamcoat

Streetwise-crackers: the city's top club comedians, including Stevie Faye and Mickey Finn, promote an all-star charity do in the 1970s

Coining it – counting the results of the 'pennies on the drum' effort after the Old Town Hall show at The Empire in September 1942, Gladys and Clay Keyes, with C. Denier Warren and members of the WAAF

Liverpool's dance halls were regularly beamed across the land when Come Dancing came to film the inter-regional dance-offs

Bernard Duggan is 80-years-old now, but back in 1954 he was king of the dancefloor. Bernard, from Wirral, shared these wonderful photographs of his time with the dance display teams at The Grafton.

He says: "I am eighty now but I won't forget the dancing back then in 1954. Great days for all of us. I was a dance fanatic – still am. From Kensington, Fairfield to The Grafton.

"Looking back on these photographs, kept in a box and now in a magazine, it all comes back...the music and the dance, the atmosphere and elegance. The one and only, legendary Victor Sylvester also played there.

"I collected and kept these pictures and memories and they still make me smile."

"The music and dance, the atmosphere and elegance"

The Grafton has hosted famous bandleaders, including Victor Sylvester, pictured here, and below, in 1954

"When I grow up,
I want to dance like
my brother.
Who looks dead
smart in his
flowery shirt and
flared pants,
And my big sis
in her mini-skirt
(But why did my dad call
her nothing but 'a flirt'?)
I'll be a dancer,
I know.
'Cos I'm no good at
sports, but I was the star
of the school disco.
I want to
mess around
again on the
village hall floor,
have pints of
orange juice,
Then dance and
dance and dance
some more..."

Strictly Ambitious in the summer of 1970 – youngsters gather at the Top Rank Suite, Liverpool, to do the latest dance to music supplied by DJ Bobby Dean

"Tankards for the memory in honour of blue and red world class stars"

Gerry Byrne, Ray Wilson, Ian Callaghan and Roger Hunt with their tankards presented to them by the Lord Mayor of Liverpool in recognition for their selection for England's World Cup Squad in 1966

Photo shoot – an Everton team shot by ace soccer-snapper Stephen Shakeshaft in the late 1960s

'Up the reds' was their battle cry, as these Liverpool supporters made themselves seen and heard at Blackburn for an FA Cup fixture in 1958

Fan-tastic: Liverpool's red army fly out to join 1,000 other fans in Belgium for the EUFA Cup final against AC Bruges, May 1976. Stan Boardman was upset we weren't playing the Germans...

Left, Roy Vernon and Sandy Brown with koala bear mascots, souvenirs of the successful Everton FC close season tour of Australia in 1964. Right, Everton Toffee girl Joanne Francis and her sister Gillian, responsible for giving out about 4lb of the traditional Barker and Dobson Everton toffees before every home game in 1983

Red Rum offers postman Ken Sykes a few tips as he delivers a parcel to the three-times National winner in April, 1989 – but how is Rummy going to get that string undone?

Motor mania – the line-up at the start of the great European Grand Prix race at Aintree in July 1957

Motorcycle racing fans queue at Liverpool Landing Stage for the Isle of Man steamer, in readiness for the T.T. races, June 1976

The last hurdle: Olympic dreams at Merchant Taylors' School in March 1951

Marathon Day in September 1982, as more than 5,000 runners tackle the 26-mile route from Sefton Park to Bootle and back

Geoff Capes takes on four American footballers in a friendly tug-of-war, with a little local help, at the opening of Tasker's sports store in Utting Avenue, June 1986

Boys from the Gordon Institute Lads' Club at a training event at St George's Hall in May 1951

Jubilant nurses celebrate VE-Day in 1945

Church Street, Liverpool, circa 1960 – you can almost smell the Kardomah coffee and hear the laughter from the Tatler Cartoon Cinema in those pre-pedestrianisation days

"It may be just another memory.
Don't let it slip away.
A picture postcard,
A dream,
An unexpected bouquet.
Don't let go of what has been, of what you've heard,
Of what you've seen."

Betty Horne and her mother Ellen Prior, who ran the florist's shop overlooking the Rotunda site on Scottie Road, 1970

"We're all in it together..."

A strike meeting in 1945 and 1,000 dockers who were unable to gain admission to branch headquarters in Brasenose Road, Liverpool

No, it isn't work on the third Mersey tunnel, but one of the first A.R.P. steel shelters goes up in 1939 at St Mary's Gardens, Mulberry Street, Liverpool

Champagne for Jack Smith, manager of Ma Boyle's Oyster Bar in 1974, as he says farewell to the original premises on Old Hall Street and barmaids Francis, Mary and Sadie

Traffic negotiates the new one-way system in Shaw Street in 1965

The heatwave of 1976. A hosepipe ban didn't stop kids enjoying this flood on Prescot Road, outside the Lord Nelson pub

First come, first served at Birkenhead Market, 1965

The crowded decks of the North Wales steamer St Tudno as she departs Liverpool in the 1950s

The 'People's Princess' at ease with workers in the Ford Halewood upholstery section, September 1988

Excitement never flagged. Nearly everyone was making waves during Princess Margaret's visit to Southport in May 1954

"Lookin' good, kid"
"Feelin' fine, son!"